You Are There

Transportation

From Cars to Planes

By Gare Thompson

CHILDREN'S PRESS®
A Division of Grolier Publishing
New York • London • Hong Kong • Sydney
Danbury, Connecticut

D1316818

Reading Consultant	Linda Cornwell, Learning Resource Consultant, Indiana Department of Education

Acknowledgments:

Product Development	Gare Thompson Associates
Design	Carlos Gaudier
Production	Silver Editions
Editor	Beverly Mitchell
Research	Donald Mitchell

Photo Credits:

Cover (top left, top right), Images © 1996 PhotoDisc, Inc.;cover (top center), (Corbis-Bettman; cover (bottom left), © Library of Congress; cover (bottom right), © NASA; 3 (top left), Images © 1996 PhotoDisc, Inc.; 3 (top right), © NASA; 4 (left), © Bonnie Spring/Stock Boston; 4 (right), © Library of Congress; 5 (left, right), © Library of Congress; 6 (center) (UPI/Corbis-Bettman; 6 (right), © Library of Congress; 7 © Bryce Flynn/Stock Boston; 8 (left), © Library of Congress; 8(right), © Edith Lee Francis; 9 (left), © Library of Congress; 9 (right), © Ford Motor Co.; 10 (left), © Greig Cranna/Stock Boston; 10 (right), © Mark C. Burnett/Stock Boston; 11 (left), © Ena Keo/Photographer; 11 (right), © Bryce Flynn/Stock Boston; 12 (left), © Library of Congress; 12 (right), © Ford Motor Co.; 13 © Library of Congress; 14 (left), © Judith Canty/Stock Boston; 14 (right), © Whaling Museum/New Bedford, Mass.; 15 (left, right), © Library of Congress; 16 (left), © Bettman Archives; 16 (right), © Library of Congress; 17 (left), © John Elk III/Stock Boston; 17 (right), Images © 1996 PhotoDisc, Inc.; 18 (left), © Bettman Archives; 18 (center), © Library of Congress; 18 (right), © Library of Congress; 19 © Library of Congress; 20 (left, right), © Library of Congress; 21 (left), © Northern Pacific Railway; 21 (right), © Library of Congress; 22 (left), © Library of Congress; 22 (right), © Peter Southwick/Stock Boston; 23 (left), © Dallas & John Heaton/Stock Boston; 23 (center), © Ena Keo/Photographer; 23 (right), © David Ulmer/Stock Boston; 24 (left, right), © Library of Congress; 25 © Library of Congress; 26 (left, right), © Library of Congress; 27 (left, right), © Library of Congress;28 (left), Images © 1996 PhotoDisc, Inc.; 28 (right), © Bettman Archives; 29 (left), © Richard Pasley/Stock Boston; 29 (right), © NASA; 30 © Library of Congress; 31 Images © 1996 PhotoDisc, Inc.

Library of Congress Cataloging–in–Publication Data

Thompson, Gare.

   Transportation / Gare Thompson.

     p. cm. — (You are there)

   Includes bibliographical refererces (p.).

   Summary: Surveys different modes of transportation, such as automobiles, ships, trains, and planes, and discusses their development in history.

   ISBN 0-516-20705-9 (lib. bdg.)   0-516-26055-3 (pbk.)

   1. Transportation—History—Juvenile literature.

[1. Transportation—History.] I. Title. II. Series: You are there (Danbury, Conn.)

TA1149.T48 1997

629.04--dc21   96-52027

                                                 CIP

                                                 AC

Transportation

Cars take us to work and play. Trains move everything from apples to zinc. Ships bring food and goods to harbor cities. Planes take us to faraway places. Rockets take us to the moon. How do you think we will travel in the future?

Three Inventions...

The Wheel

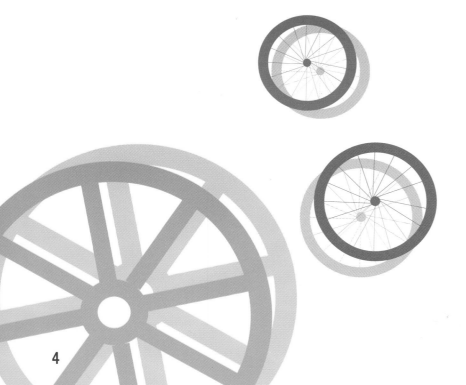

First, people had to think about easier ways to move things. Maybe someone saw a rock roll down a hill and thought of rolling logs to move heavy things. Soon the wheel was invented.

Wheels were attached to wagons. Horses pulled the wagons. These wagons could carry heavy loads. They moved people and goods long distances. Roads were built to make travel easier. Roads connected towns and cities.

Sailing Ships

Sailing ships moved people and goods. Early ships used huge sails and the wind for power. Ships carried people and goods along rivers and across oceans. Ports, where ships loaded and unloaded goods, grew to be important cities.

Steam Engines

Steam engines were invented in the 1700s. James Watt used steam engines to power ships. Steamships could travel farther faster. But they could not travel across the land.

...Made Transportation Possible

Trains, Cars, and Planes...

Trains

Next, trains were invented. Trains used steam engines for power. Trains carried people and goods across the United States. Railroads were the best way to ship goods for almost 100 years. As railroad tracks were built, towns and jobs grew up around them.

Cars

Before long, the first car was built. Early cars also used steam engines. Cars soon replaced most trains as a way for people to travel. Cars were cheaper and faster to travel short distances. By 1928, many families owned cars.

Planes

While most people were learning to drive, other people dreamed of flying. After many tries, the Wright brothers finally flew an airplane for less than a minute. Later, planes flew across the ocean and around the world.

Now we have fast cars, ships, trains, planes, and even space ships, because of three important inventions.

Transportation has made the world easier to explore. Where shall we go and how will we get there?

Cars

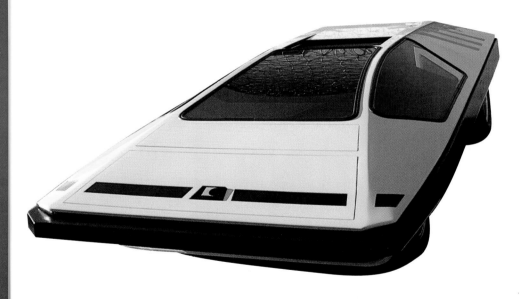

Carts and wagons once moved people and goods. Then bikes moved people. Now cars move us. More and different kinds of cars are being built every day. What would our lives be like if cars had not been invented?

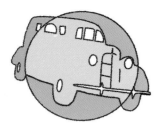

timeline

1860

1880

In the 1860s, people traveled west in stagecoaches.

Police often used bicycles on patrol in cities.

Westward-Ho, Wagons on the Move!

Wagons moved many people. Stagecoaches and Conestoga wagons carried settlers west. Sometimes the wagons were too heavy to climb over mountains, so families had to leave their belongings along the way.

Bone-Shaking Bicycles

Bicycles also moved people. They were cheaper than cars. Early bicycles had hard metal wheels. When people rode them, their bones really shook! Rubber wheels made bicycles easier to ride.

First Came the Wheel and Then Came the Car

1900

Horse-drawn carts delivered milk in the 1890s.

Wagons Everywhere

In cities, wagons delivered milk, ice, and goods to homes. Wagons were everywhere. Fire wagons carried water to put out fires. Fancy wagons carried people to dances and parties.

1920

A Mechanical Horse: the Car

Early cars were called horseless carriages. By the 1920s, Henry Ford's assembly line produced many cars. The Model T Fords all looked alike. Cars soon replaced wagons.

Cars rolling off an assembly line

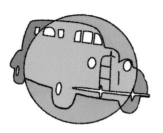

1940

1960

Cars Everywhere

Cars were everywhere by the 1940s. Highways were built to link cities to the countryside. People drove cars to work. Families drove cars on vacation.

All Kinds of Cars

By 1960 there was a car for everyone. People wanted different kinds of cars. Some were sporty, some were fancy, and some were plain. Building these cars created many jobs. People could pick a car just for them.

By the late 1940s, most American families were driving cars.

Cars Change the Way We Live

1980

Back to Bicycles

People began using bicycles again. They wanted to slow the pollution caused by cars. Today bikes are used for many things. Bikes now deliver food and people.

Here is a modern bicycle taxi.

2000

Into the Future

Cars continue to change. They look very different from the Model T Ford. What do you think cars will look like in the year 2020?

Will cars look like this in the future?

Did you know?

In 1927 a Model T Ford cost around $250. Today most cars cost more than $10,000.

Henry Ford

GENTLEMEM OUR COUNTRY

Henry Ford was born on July 30, 1863. He lived on a farm near Dearborn, Michigan. Henry did not like farming, but he loved fixing machinery.

Ford began building a car in 1890 and finished his first car in 1896. In 1903, he started the Ford Motor Company. He said, "The way to make automobiles is to make . . . them all alike." And that is what he did. Today, Ford is one of the largest car companies in the world. Henry Ford died on April 7, 1947.

Ships

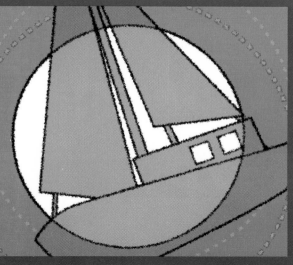

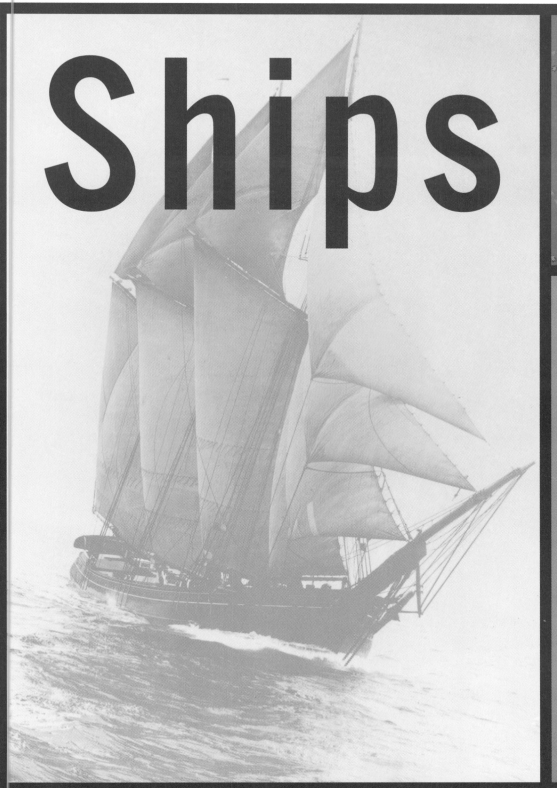

Three-quarters of the Earth is water. Ships carry people and goods across water. Ships travel on rivers, canals, lakes, and oceans. Ships move people and goods around the world. But what are the different kinds of ships we use?

timeline

1700	1800

Canoes

Native Americans built canoes. They used canoes to fish and to travel places. Canoes were made from hollowed-out logs and birchbark. Canoes are still used today.

Whaling Ships

Whaling ships hunted for whales. Whales had many uses. Whales provided oil for lamps, bones for making tools, and blubber for food. Today it is not legal to hunt for whales.

People used canoes to travel on rivers and lakes.

Whaling ships traveled for many months to find whales.

Many Kinds of Ships

1830

Clipper ships had huge sails to catch the wind.

Clipper Ships Sail the World

Clipper ships were large and fast sailing ships. They were called moonrakers. Clipper ships sailed to Asia to trade silks and spices. They sailed in the 1830s and 1840s. Ships powered by steam took the place of clipper ships. Steamships could travel faster and farther than clipper ships.

1870

Steamships

A famous race took place on July 4, 1870. The *Robert E. Lee* challenged the *Natchez* to a race on the Mississippi River. They raced from Vicksburg, Mississippi, to New Orleans, Louisiana. The *Robert E. Lee* won. It made the trip in 3 days, 18 hours, and 14 minutes. Steamships became the rulers of rivers.

The steamboat race

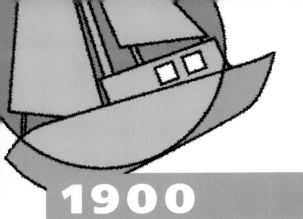

1900

Cruise Ships

Cruise ships were popular in the early 1900s. They were like floating hotels.

The Olympic White Star Line built the largest cruise ship in 1911. It had a very large swimming pool, bronze lamps, and marble drinking fountains. It held over 2,500 passengers.

The grand salon of a luxury liner

1930

Fishing Boats

For centuries, men on boats have searched the lakes, seas, and oceans for fish. Fishing became a very big industry in the 1930s and 1940s. Today, fishing boats have the best equipment to keep the fishermen safe and to bring us fresh seafood.

This is a fishing boat from the 1940s.

1960

1990

Freighters bring goods to and from many different ports.

Freighters

Huge ships carry freight around the world. Freighters are built to make loading and unloading easy. Port cities such as New Orleans, Boston, Savannah, New York, Baltimore, and San Francisco have harbors where freighters can load and unload goods.

Hydrofoils and Speedboats

Hydrofoils float on a thrust of air just above the water. These high-speed boats carry people across rivers, bays, channels, and other rough water. Speedboats are very popular today, too. They carry children to school and are used as police cruisers on water.

Speedboats today are very fast.

MEET:

Robert Fulton

Robert Fulton was born on November 14, 1765. He worked as an artist, inventor, and engineer. Fulton planned and built a submarine in 1800. No one would buy it so he decided to build better steamboats.

In 1807, Fulton launched a steamboat, the Clermont, in New York harbor. He built a very successful steamboat business. He also invented a power shovel to dig canals to connect lakes, rivers, and oceans, where steamboats were used. Robert Fulton died on February 24, 1815.

Did you know?

One famous ship, the Titanic, was built to be unsinkable. In April, 1912, on its first trip from England to New York it hit an iceberg and sank.

Trains

The first railroad engines were . . . horses! They pulled wagons along wooden tracks. They were replaced by steam engines, called iron horses, and steel rails. How do we use trains today?

timeline

1830

1860

Laying Tracks

In 1830, the first train in the United States ran near Baltimore, Maryland, on 13 miles of track. Soon, tracks connected many cities and towns.

On the first trains, people sat in open cars, brought food to eat, and slept sitting up. Later, the cars were covered, and trains had dining and sleeping cars.

A steam train ran from Albany, New York, to Schenectedy, New York, in 1832.

Many workers came from China to build the railroads.

New Jobs!

Railroads created jobs. Many people worked to build the railroads. Others worked as engineers, firemen, porters, ticket clerks, and mechanics to keep the trains running. People in nearby towns sold food and clothing to the workers. People also came from faraway to build the tracks.

the Iron Horses of the 1800's

1875

East Meets West

On May 10, 1869, railroad tracks from the east and the west were joined by a golden spike at Promontory Point, Utah. By 1885, trains could deliver goods from coast to coast within a week!

East meets West.

1890

Big Trains and Fast Locomotives

Big Boy engines pulled the largest trains ever built. They weighed more than 500 tons and pulled 5,000-ton trains over the Rocky Mountains.

Locomotive 999 set a world speed record of 112 miles per hour. It had a cow catcher in front to push cows off the tracks.

Locomotive 999 set the record in 1893.

1920

Freight Trains

Freight trains carried all kinds of goods. Cars, furniture, food, and grain were carried in boxcars. Refrigerator cars carried fruit and meat. Tank cars carried milk, oil, and chemicals. Open slat cars carried cows and chickens. Flat cars carried building supplies.

Freight trains carried goods to cities and towns.

1950

Passenger Trains

In the 1950s, many people traveled by train for business and pleasure. Passenger trains had coaches with comfortable seats, dining cars with cooks and waiters, and sleeping cars with beds.

Passenger trains make long trips across North America.

22

1980

Bullet trains travel at high speeds.

Fast Trains

In Japan and Europe, bullet trains race along at up to 160 miles per hour. The train tracks are tilted or banked around curves to allow such high speeds.

2000

RAILROAD CROSSING

Tomorrow's Trains

Today, airplane travel is faster than train travel. But there are still some pretty fast trains! How fast do you think trains will travel in the future?

How fast will trains travel in the future?

Railroads became acceptable once Queen Victoria of England and U.S. President James Polk rode on trains.

MEET:

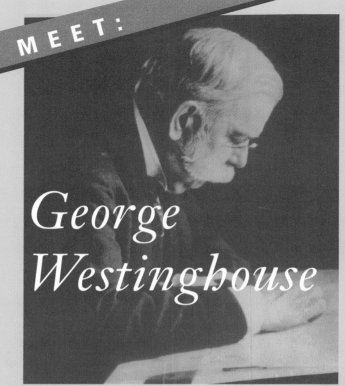

George Westinghouse

George Westinghouse was born in Central Bridge, New York, on October 6, 1846. As a boy, George loved playing with tools and inventing things. He wanted to know how everything worked.

Westinghouse loved trains, but he thought they were not safe. He invented the air brake, interlocking switches, and a complete railroad signaling system. These inventions made railroads much safer. During his lifetime, Westinghouse invented over 400 items. George Westinghouse died on March 12, 1914.

Planes

We have always wanted to fly, soaring like birds up in the sky. Airplanes take us to faraway places quickly. Rockets explore new frontiers in outer space. Where will we go next?

timeline

1880

Early Flight

People tried to fly using feathered wings, balloons, and gliders. Hot-air balloons proved that people could move through the air. Gliders, using wind power, taught people how wings worked. Samuel P. Langley began his experiments in flight in the 1800s. By 1896 he had built a model airplane which flew half a mile without a passenger.

This early airplane could only stay up in the air for a few minutes.

1900

The Wright brothers fly their plane.

The First Manned Flight

Orville and Wilbur Wright flew a plane on December 17, 1903. Their plane, the *Flyer*, flew for 12 seconds in Kitty Hawk, North Carolina. They made three more flights that day. The longest one was 59 seconds. The Wright brothers became famous.

Flying like the birds

1920

Lindbergh checks his plane before flying to Paris.

Lindbergh Does It!

In 1927, Charles Lindbergh designed and built a special airplane to fly across the Atlantic Ocean.

1940

A flying boat

Floating Ships: Landing on the Water

In the 1930s and 1940s, some passenger planes were known as flying boats. They were like large cruise ships, and they landed on water. They carried 74 passengers and a crew of ten. It took almost 24 hours to fly across the Atlantic Ocean.

Up, Up and away

1960

Leaving on a Jet Plane

Jets planes fly people and goods around the world. Many people travel to faraway places for work and for vacations. Planes can carry goods across oceans much faster than ships.

Many jets can hold over 200 people.

1975

Around the World in No Time

Some jets can fly to Europe in less than four hours. The Concorde travels at 1,320 miles per hour. It passes through the sound barrier.

The Concorde is a supersonic passenger plane.

1990

Airplanes Today

Modern planes can hold many passengers and fly all over the world. Pilots and their crews are highly trained. Airplanes use radar to see where they are flying. Computers are used to fly the planes. Planes need huge airports to take off and land.

In airports, computer screens tell people when planes are coming and going.

2000

Flight into Space

Now rockets explore outer space. They are finding new planets. Soon, a new spacecraft may go anywhere on Earth in about an hour. It would take off like a jet plane, soar into space like a rocket, and then land like a plane. Do you think this will happen?

Space shuttles help us learn about space and other planets.

Did you know?

While crossing the English channel in a balloon, John Jeffries and Jean-Pierre Blanchard began sinking. They had to throw out as much as they could, including their clothes. They landed in Paris in their underwear!

Charles Lindbergh

Charles Lindbergh was born on February 4, 1902, in Detroit, Michigan. Charles wanted to fly. He began by flying mail planes.

There was a contest to fly alone across the Atlantic Ocean. The prize was $25,000. Lindbergh designed a special plane, the *Spirit of St. Louis.* On May 20, 1927, Lindbergh left Roosevelt Field, New York. He arrived in Paris, France, on May 21st. His flight took thirty-three hours and thirty-nine minutes. He flew across the Atlantic alone. Lindbergh returned home a hero. He died on August 26, 1974.

How will we travel in the future?

Transportation has changed the world.

We can now travel faster and farther than ever before. We can buy goods from around the world. We even travel into space and beyond. How does transportation affect you?

Learn More About Transportation

Here are some additional resources to help you learn more about transportation.

Books

Donnelly, J. **The Titanic Lost . . . and Found**. 1987. Random House

English, June. **Transportation: Automobiles to Zeppelins**. 1995. Scholastic.

McMillan, Bruce. **Grandfather's Trolley**. 1995. Candlewick.

Micklethwait, Lucy. **I Spy a Freight Train**. 1996. Greenwillow Books.

Parlin, John. **Amelia Earhart: Pioneer in the Sky**. 1991. Dell.

Shea, George. **First Flight: The Story of Tom Tate and the Wright Brothers**. 1997. HarperCollins.

Video

Cars, Boats, Trains, Planes. 1986. Warner Reprise Video.

CD-ROM

Oregon Trail II. 1994. MECC.

Interactive exploration of the history and geography of the Old West.

Online Sites

National Aeronautics and Space Administration
   http://www.nasa.gov
   Investigate facts about NASA and the space program.

Smithsonian Institution
   http://www.si.edu
   Explore historical information about all kinds of transportation.

U.S. Department of Transportation
   http://www.dot.gov
   Research facts and statistics about transportation.